Ships

by Cari Meister

Bullfrog Books

Ideas for Parents and Teachers

Bullfrog Books let children practice nonfiction reading at the earliest reading levels. Repetition, familiar words, and photo labels support early readers.

Before Reading

- Discuss the cover photo. What does it tell them?
- Look at the picture glossary together. Read and discuss the words.

Read the Book

- "Walk" through the book and look at the photos. Let the child ask questions. Point out the photo labels.
- Read the book to the child, or have him or her read independently.

After Reading

- Prompt the child to think more. Ask: What kinds of ships have you seen? What jobs were they doing?

Bullfrog Books are published by Jump!
5357 Penn Avenue South
Minneapolis, MN 55419
www.jumplibrary.com

Library of Congress Cataloging-in-Publication Data
Meister, Cari.
Ships / by Cari Meister.
p. cm. -- (Machines at work)
Summary: "This photo-illustrated book for early readers tells about the parts of a ship and different kinds of ships used for transportation of goods and people"--Provided by publisher.
Includes bibliographical references and index.
Audience: K-3.
ISBN 978-1-62031-047-2 (alk. paper) -- ISBN 978-1-62496-059-8 (ebk.)
1. Shipping--Juvenile literature. 2. Ships--Juvenile literature. I. Title.
HE571.M378 2014
623.82--dc23 2012042020

Series Editor: Rebecca Glaser
Book Editor: Patrick Perish
Series Designer: Ellen Huber
Book Designer: Sara Pokorny

Photo Credits:
Alamy, 6, 12, 22bl; Dreamstime, 3, 4, 11; iStock, 22, 23bl, 24; Shutterstock, cover, 1, 5, 7, 8, 9, 10, 13, 14–15, 16, 17, 18–19, 20b, 20t, 21, 22br, 23tl, 23br, 23tr

Printed in the United States of America at Corporate Graphics in North Mankato, Minnesota.
5-2013 / PO 1003

10 9 8 7 6 5 4 3 2 1

Table of Contents

Ships at Work

BROOONG!

The horn sounds.
A ship goes out to sea.

How does it move?

It has a big engine.
It powers the ship.

propeller

A ship has steel propellers.
They spin fast.
They make the ship go.

The captain steers the ship.

He is up on the bridge.

He can see all around.

bridge

DOLE EUROPA
Dole

A ship carries fruit.
It has coolers on board.
They keep food fresh.

A tanker carries gas.
It is stored in round tanks.

tank

A carrier holds airplanes.
The deck is a runway.

Whoosh!

A fishing ship is far out at sea.

Its crane lifts big nets.

crane

All aboard!

A family goes on a trip.

They take a cruise ship.

Have fun!

Parts of a Ship

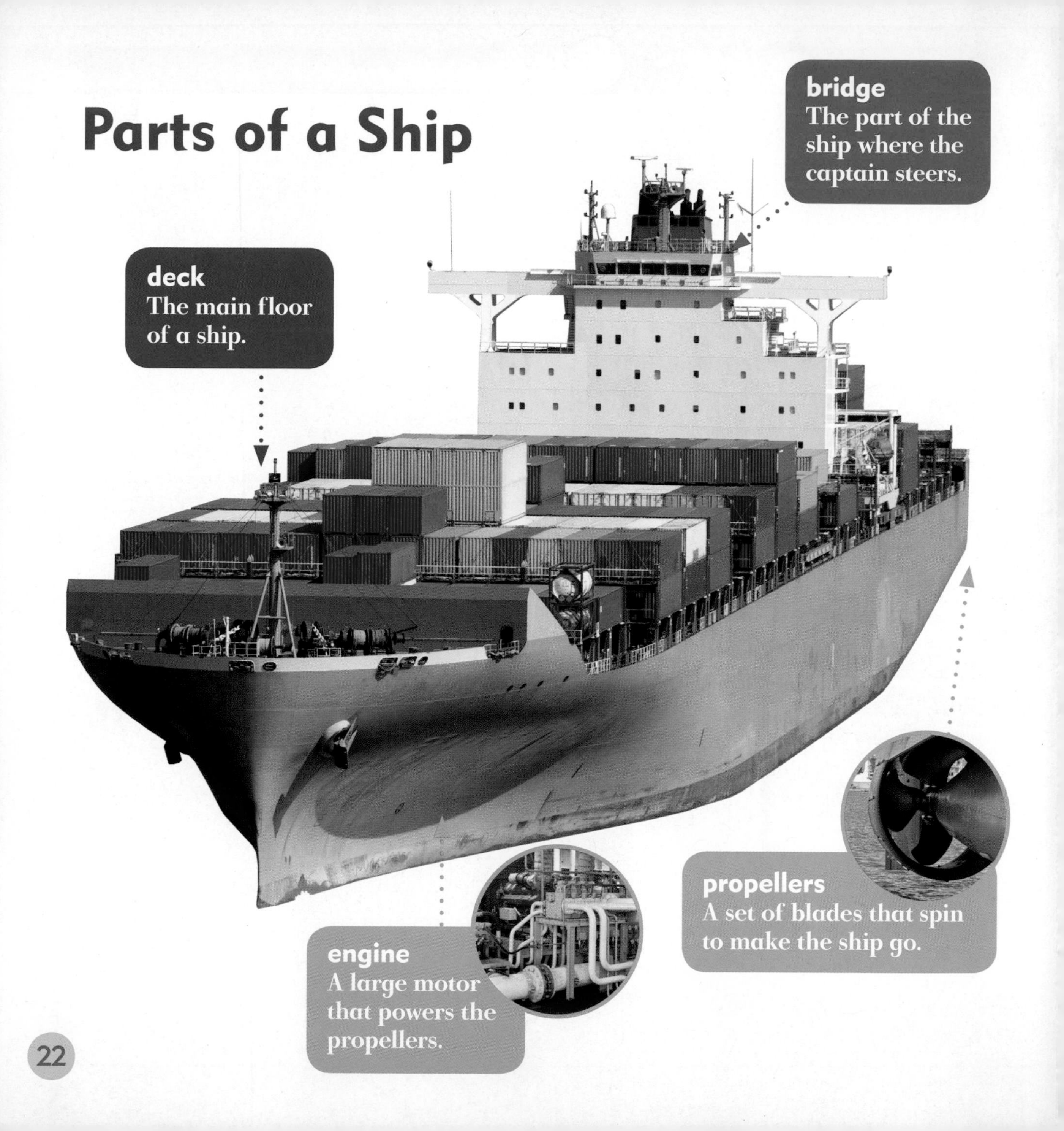

Picture Glossary

carriers
Ships that carry airplanes; they are also called aircraft carriers.

crane
A large machine that has an arm used for lifting heavy things.

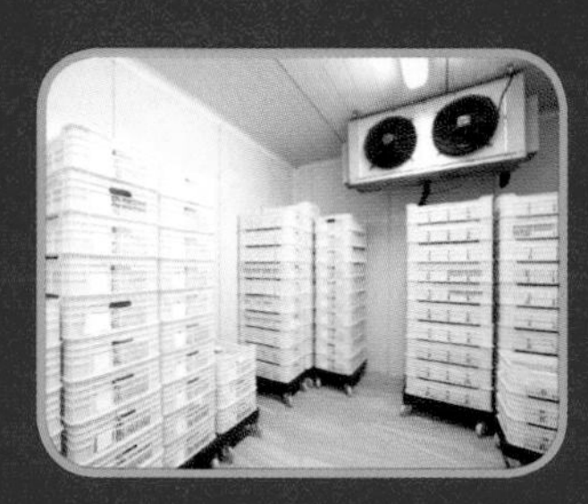

coolers
Big rooms on ships that are cold to keep food fresh; they are like giant refrigerators.

tankers
Ships that carry liquids, like liquid gas.

Index

To Learn More

Learning more is as easy as 1, 2, 3.

1) Go to www.factsurfer.com

2) Enter "ship" into the search box.

3) Click the "Surf" button to see a list of websites.

With factsurfer.com, finding more information is just a click away.